HELP YOUR YOUNG CHILD TO SUCCEED

The essential guide for parents of 3–5 year olds

Ros Bayley, Lynn Broadbent
and Debbie Pullinger

Family Learning

Series editor: Bill Lucas

Published by Network Continuum Education
The Tower Building
11 York Road
London
SE1 7NX

www.networkcontinuum.co.uk
www.continuumbooks.com

An imprint of The Continuum International Publishing Group Ltd

First published 2006
© Ros Bayley, Lynn Broadbent and Debbie Pullinger 2006

ISBN-13: 978 185539 214 4
ISBN-10:   185539 214 3

Managing editor: Debbie Pullinger
Design by: Neil Hawkins, ndesign
Illustration by: Margaret Chamberlain and Ian Dicks

Printed in Great Britain by Ashford Colour Press Ltd., Gosport, Hants.

CONTENTS

Introduction

If your child is between the ages of three and five, you'll know that life with a young child can be interesting, exciting, boring, frustrating, entertaining, delightful, surprising, maddening and exhausting. Yet these years are crucial ones in a child's development. At this time, perhaps more than at any other, you have the opportunity to make a big difference to your child's chances of success in life. The aim of this book, which is part of the Help Your Child series, is to help you to make that difference.

Children at this stage can be in all sorts of quite different situations. There are those who have begun their full-time education and those whose care and education is still entirely within the sphere of home with a parent or other relative. There are those who spend a few hours a week in a pre-school setting of some kind, and those who have been in day care since before their first birthday. Nevertheless, there are certain things that all children of this age need. So we hope that whatever your particular circumstances, you will find plenty of ideas to try.

Each chapter begins with a few questions to introduce some of the ideas that will be covered. These are followed by a **Quiz**, which in many chapters gets you looking back at your own experience of childhood. What we do as parents is always affected by our own experience of being parented. Reflecting on that experience can provide helpful insights into what we are doing with our own children, and help to sort out our ideas about what we would like to do.

The **Quick check** at the end of each chapter provides a reminder of the key points.

The **Resources** section at the back offers a list of suggestions for books and CDs to enjoy with your child, plus details of useful websites. Where you see **W** on a page, this indicates that there is a related website address in the Resources section.

Finally, we have chosen to use 'he' and 'she' in alternate chapters, and what we say applies equally to both – except where we've said otherwise!

Your Child, Your Family

Did you know...

? A lot of 'hard wiring' in a child's brain happens in the first five years of life?

? Parents are a child's most important teachers?

? It's the home, not the school, that really determines how well children learn?

? No matter what your intelligence or level of ability, when you give your child your time and attention you will be helping him to learn?

> I consider the period from age two to age six... a fascinating period of human development... it harbors more of the secrets and power of human growth than any other comparable phase. *Howard Gardner*

WHAT WAS IT LIKE TO BE A CHILD?

Can you remember what it was like to be a young child? Have you ever thought about how your childhood affects what sort of parent you are?

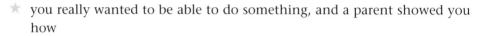

Take a few moments to remember. How did your parents treat you as a young child? What was it like for you when:

- ★ a parent spent time with you

- ★ a parent was not able to spend time with you

- ★ you learned something new – like how to ride a bike

- ★ you really wanted to be able to do something, and a parent showed you how

- ★ you helped with cooking or household jobs

- ★ someone read you a bedtime story

- ★ you couldn't understand something, and a parent explained it to you

- ★ a parent was waiting by the school gates and you ran out to show them something you had done or made – did you get a smile and praise, or some other response

- ★ a parent got angry or upset with you, or said something to put you down?

Like it or not, our experience of childhood – whether happy or otherwise – affects how we respond to our own children.

Can you see how your experience might influence the way you respond to your own child?

Do you treat your own child in the same way as your parents treated you – or do you try to do things differently?

Do you try to do things differently but find yourself doing exactly the same?

If possible, chat about your experience with a partner or a friend.

Being the parent of a young child

If your child has reached or is coming up to the age of three, you'll probably have noticed by now that:

- Children are very hard work.
- Whatever good intentions you started out with, it's all too easy to get bogged down in the day-to-day business of keeping the show on the road.
- It's never the same game two years running (or sometimes two months running). No sooner have you worked out how to deal with one stage, than he's onto the next.
- What works for someone else's child may not necessarily work for yours.
- It's very easy to spend a lot of time worrying and feeling inadequate and guilty.

Being a young child

When we say three to five years, that's just a rough guide. What we're talking about here is children who are past the wobbly toddler stage but still very dependent on you and their special grown-ups. Abilities and rate of development in this age group vary enormously, but your child is probably someone who:

is rapidly acquiring physical skills

can hold a conversation – and asks endless questions

enjoys simple games

likes to hear stories – and invents his own

wants independence – but still needs safety and security

is growing in courage and confidence.

Growing and learning together

If you recognize this picture of life with a young child, the good news is that your child – like all young children – is in the business of learning. As a parent, you can make a real difference to the quality of that learning and influence the sort of person your child will become.

Recent TV programmes have focused attention on the challenges of being a parent, and the child experts are full of genuinely helpful advice. But they can also leave us feeling that parenting is a job full of problems that require an 'expert' to solve. Plus, an hour-long programme can create the impression that all problems are quickly fixed – whereas in real-life time, results may take rather longer.

However, the truth is that you are the expert on your child. Of course, you have to work out how you, as a parent, will respond to him – and that takes some learning on your part. In the past, a lot of that learning would have come through experience within a family or local community, but the shape of modern life means that many of us no longer have that experience and just have to learn 'on the job' – perhaps with the help of TV programmes and books like this one! But we can learn – even as adults. The rest of this book is intended to help you do just that, as you and your child learn together.

To get the most from this book...

- **Take it one step at a time**. Don't feel you have to tackle everything at once. If you do, you'll almost certainly feel like giving up straight away. Begin with an idea that inspires you – or with a strategy you can imagine making a real difference.

- **Be a learner yourself**. It makes things easier if you have a positive attitude towards new ways of doing things and don't get hung up about making mistakes. And if you can adopt an attitude of learning as you go through life, your child will learn to be a learner by example.

- **Be creative in your approach**. Parents, children and families come in all shapes and sizes, and there is no one-size-fits-all way of being a parent. So find what works for you and your child.

Did you know...

? Success in life does not depend only on academic ability?

? You can be a positive influence on your child's developing personality?

? Learning involves feeling as well as thinking?

? Our attitude to mistakes makes all the difference to how we learn?

" What a child doesn't receive he can seldom later give. *PD James* "

WHAT DO YOU WANT FOR YOUR CHILD?

What would you like for your child?
How would you like her to turn out?

Take a few moments to look at the words
below and circle the five characteristics you
would most like your child to have. Then draw
a line through those you definitely do not want
her to have.

adventurous   athletic   artistic   questioning

fearful   sociable   kind   independent   obedient

loving   energetic   positive   quiet   self-confident

sensitive   receptive   risk-taking   timid   versatile   creative   talkative

well-adjusted   emotional   sense of humour   careful   conforming

stubborn   domineering   critical   courteous   competitive   courageous

negative   industrious   persevering   conforming   rebellious   refined

adaptable   resilient   problem-solving   resourceful   co-operative

thoughtful   responsible   empathetic   determined   purposeful

Now look carefully at your choices and, if possible, compare your answers with
your partner or with a friend.

The chances are that what you really want for your child does not depend
entirely on academic success. In fact, evidence shows that success in life is
not just about how clever (or how cool or good-looking or famous) you are.
There are some other characteristics that are much more important.

Look again at the choices you made. Thinking about the
things you really want for your child, how might they affect:

   ★ the way you speak to her?

   ★ the sort of conversations you have?

   ★ the experiences you let her have?

Did you know
statistics show that
despite the vast
increase in material
wealth, people in the
UK, USA and Japan are
no happier than they
were 50 years ago?

What is success?

Ask any parents what they want for their children, and most will say that they just want them to be happy and fulfilled. So what makes for a happy and fulfilled life?

Once your child has started school, it can seem as if life is one long round of tests and targets. You might well begin to think that tests and exams are the main measure of success. Of course, doing well at school and passing exams is great. But it's only one kind of success. Think about all the successful people you know. Some may have done well at school, but it's likely that some did not.

In fact, when we look at life's 'achievers', we find that their success often comes from skills and attitudes that are not tested in school, including:

maintaining self-esteem –
being comfortable with who you are; having confidence and a sense of self-worth

managing feelings –
being aware of and able to manage your own emotions

relating well to others –
being able to understand the feelings of others; to get on well with all sorts of people and to communicate effectively

staying positive –
having a positive attitude to problems and setbacks; being resourceful; being able to take risks and to see mistakes as part of the learning process

Equipped for life

These vital attitudes and skills are what will *really* equip your child for life – no matter what her intelligence or abilities. Furthermore, a child who is equipped with these 'life skills' is more likely to achieve her full potential in school. And if she gains academic success, then these skills will help her make the most of it as she goes through life. You don't need special qualifications to teach these skills. Whether you were:

a school dropout

... or top of the class

at the top of your game

... or just beginning

surfing the waves of success

... or feel a bit of a failure

... you're just the right person to help your child.

Anyone of any age can acquire these life skills. Like other skills, they can be learned and they improve with practice. But before the age of six is an especially good time to learn. This is when children are making up their minds about who they are and how they will relate to the world.

In fact, children of this age are quite literally 'making their minds up' because their brains are still developing. Put very simply, learning happens when connections are made between brain cells. And we know that a lot of the important connections – the 'hard-wiring' of the brain – are made during the first few years of life. That's not to say that we can't learn anything when we're older, but our ability to learn is shaped by what happens to us in those early years. We're also laying down the foundations of personality and self-esteem – both of which affect our ability to cope with the challenges of learning, and life in general. So this is the ideal time to help your child acquire positive attitudes and behaviour that will become part of her character – for life. In the rest of this chapter, we'll look at how you can help your child with these life skills.

Self-esteem

How we feel about ourselves makes all the difference to how we behave and what we are able to do. For young children, no one has more influence on how they feel about themselves than the adults they love.

Remember that self-esteem is not something you do and cross off the list. For all of us, self-esteem varies from day to day or even hour to hour – rather like a barometer reacting to the weather conditions.

PAUSE FOR THOUGHT: How did you feel?

Think about the last time someone told you that you did something well, or that you had done something wrong. Notice how it changed your feelings. How was the rest of the day for you?

But unlike a barometer, we accumulate the effects of positive and negative messages over time. So the more positive messages your child has, the more her self-esteem will grow. And it all starts with respect. If you have a respectful attitude towards your child, she will learn to respect herself.

Tips for learning to appreciate your child

Make a list of your child's qualities that you really like, for example:

- *I like the way Sally makes up little songs about things she's doing.*
- *I really appreciate it when she entertains her baby brother!*

Take the opportunity to tell her next time. And keep adding to the list.

Ways to boost your child's self-esteem

- **Listen to your child** – and always respect their feelings (see pages 16–17).
- **Avoid labelling** – when the hamster has escaped and chewed up your best

> You didn't close the cage properly. Next time you feed Harry, please remember to shut the door properly.

sweater because the cage wasn't closed properly, it's terribly easy to come out with something along the lines of 'You silly girl! You never think!' The danger is, however, that your child will come to believe that she really *is* silly or unthinking – or whatever. However irritated or upset you may feel, try simply to state what has happened and what you would like your child to do.

> I really liked the way you read that story – you put in all those funny voices as well !

- **Give encouragement and praise whenever you can** – and say exactly what it is you approve of.

- **Give your child jobs** – things that she will succeed in. Children of this age generally like helping with adult tasks such as cooking or cleaning. (Make the most of it while it lasts!) Being able to sort the laundry, set the table or measure out the pasta will make her feel competent and confident.

> Thirty laps – that's my best yet!

- **Be proud of your own achievements** – when your child sees you celebrating your successes, she will learn to do the same. Talk with your child about the things you think you are good at. (If your child hears you putting yourself down, she will learn that this is what you are supposed to do!)

- **Help her to have a sense of belonging** – self-esteem comes partly from a sense of belonging, so make sure your child knows about your family (and other special people) and her place in it.

ACTIVITY: Make a family board

Take photos of your child and family and friends. Make a special board or book to 'tell the story' of your family. You could include drawings and other pictures, too.

Looking at the board will help your child to see how she fits into the family and understand the relationships. When there are new friends or family members, add them in.

ACTIVITY: I can do it!

You will need: An attractive scrapbook

Every time your child does something all by herself, celebrate the occasion by recording her achievement in an 'I can do it!' book. Encourage her to talk about how she feels about her achievement, and record her comments in the book. Draw pictures with her and add a photograph and a date.

You might include: riding a bike, buttoning her coat, tying her own shoelaces, writing her own name.

This will help your child to see herself as a capable person who is able to take care of her own needs and learn new things. As she looks back through the book she will remember these moments, and this will help her understanding of the passing of time.

Did you know that shared family rules will create a sense of belonging?

Feelings

There is a lot of talk these days about **emotional intelligence** – with good reason. Research has produced strong evidence that emotions play a far bigger part in our thinking, learning and behaviour than most people appreciate. In other words, we cannot separate our rational thinking from our emotions.

So it really does help if we pay attention to our feelings, and learn how to understand and manage them. In fact, as you may realize, there's really nothing new about emotional intelligence. It's only what lots of good parents have tried to teach their children all along.

PAUSE FOR THOUGHT: the power of feeling

Think about the last time you were angry or upset about something. You may notice how it was hard to think clearly about the situation at the time. This is because our 'emotional brain' can actually overpower our 'thinking brain', so it becomes difficult to think rationally. Then we have to be careful not to do things we might later regret!

The language of feelings

The starting point for managing feelings is being aware of them. Young children are often more in touch with their feelings than we are as adults, but they may need help to identify and talk about them. It will help your child if you are able to do this yourself. Think back over the last 24 hours and notice any strong feelings that you had. Were you:

Now look back over the last 24 hours, thinking about your child. Can you name the feelings she has shown?

Dealing with feelings

Respect and value *all* of your child's emotions – including the negative ones. Remember, all feelings are real for the person who has them. Saying 'I'm sure it's not that bad – you don't have to cry about it' may leave her confused and even guilty about what she's feeling. Eventually, she may come to believe that if she shows how she is really feeling, she won't be accepted and loved. When your child is angry or upset, try this:

1. First, remind yourself that this isn't a problem that you need to fix as soon as possible, but an opportunity for you both to learn.

2. Find out what has happened, and help your child to say how she is feeling.

3. Acknowledge her feelings and encourage her to talk about them. Listen really carefully, and try to understand the situation from her point of view. Try not to tell her how you think she should feel.

4. Talk about the problem, and together find a solution. You may need to set limits and suggest alternatives.

- It may seem surprising, but one of the best ways of calming a child who is upset is simply to acknowledge her feelings. It may feel as if you are adding fuel to the fire, but just letting her know that she has been heard can help her start to feel better and begin to deal with the problem.

- It's very tempting to feel that you have to sort out every problem for your child. But if you do, it will be hard for her to learn independence and the ability to deal with problems herself.

Dealing with tantrums

Some children seem to specialize in this particular form of parent torture. First, remember that your child is throwing a tantrum because she hasn't got things quite her way, and she hasn't learned any other way of dealing with that. So:

- Whatever you do, don't give in to her demand. She will then learn that throwing a tantrum is the perfect way to get exactly what she wants.

- Ignore the tantrum whenever possible. If you can, it may help to remove the child for a few minutes. Or remove yourself – there's no point in going on with the show if the audience has gone!

- When she's calmed down, she may need a cuddle. Then explain why she can't have or do whatever it was, and give her a choice of something else if you can.

Finally, check out your own reactions. If you explode every time something goes a teensy bit wrong … you can guess who's been taking notes!

Relating to others

Babies and toddlers cannot really appreciate anyone's point of view except their own. But from the age of about three, your child can begin to understand something of other people's thoughts and feelings.

Understanding other people's feelings

Being able to understand how other people feel is the basis of good relationships. To help your child:

- Talk about the feelings of characters in the stories you read or in TV programmes.

Poor Alfie! How do you think he felt being on his own in there?

I felt annoyed that you tore Jake's picture. How do you think Jake feels?

- Talk about your feelings when your child does something that is unkind or hurtful. Use disagreements and conflicts as a way of exploring emotions.

Katie was crying so I gived her my rabbit to cuddle, Granny.

Oh, that was a kind thing to do!

- Encourage her to be kind to others who are upset.

Good communication

To encourage good communication in your family:

- **Listen attentively**. A child who finds listening difficult will also find it difficult to learn. We learn to listen by being listened to. So make time to talk to your child and to really to listen to her (see page 67).
- **Mind your manners**. People always respond well to children who are polite. Good manners will give your child a real advantage when she goes to school and in the rest of life. The best way to instil them is to model them yourself. So try to make all requests politely, say 'thank you', and remember good manners at mealtimes!
- **Include your child in family discussions**. When discussing events or making plans, you may be surprised at how much she can contribute.

Resolving conflicts

With this approach, you are teaching your child how to resolve conflicts. It also helps her to understand that we can disagree with someone and still like and respect them.

A positive approach

There's no doubt that life can be pretty challenging. But people who are successful are generally those who have a positive attitude – a 'can do' approach to whatever life throws in their path. All of us have negative thoughts at times, but when children spend their time with adults who constantly think negatively, they fall into the same pattern.

Try to find the good in situations. When your child sees that this is what you do, she will learn to do the same. This does not mean you have to be relentlessly optimistic about everything – you'll just end up being very irritating to everyone else!

It's important to see a difficult situation for what it really is. And it's important to acknowledge how people are feeling about it (see pages 16–17). Having done that, you are then in a better position to find a way forward.

Of course, it's all too easy to fall into our usual way of responding. Changing what we say takes effort – and practice.

Try practising on these.

"It's no good, I'll never be able to set the video recorder!"

"Oh no, it's Jay – he's always moaning about something."

"I've failed the test again. I'll never be able to drive."

(See p. 96 for some ideas.)

Mind your language!

Listen to your own words. Sometimes we pass on negative attitudes without meaning to. For example:

> When you start school you will have to do really hard work!

... could give the message that school is going to be difficult and not much fun. Tune in to hear what messages you might unintentionally be giving your child. If you notice anything negative, try changing the script. For example:

> It will be really exciting and you will learn lots of new things.

... gives the more positive message that school is something to look forward to.

Mind other people's language! (within reason)

In an ideal world, you would ensure that your child spent her time with people who also gave positive messages. Of course this is just not possible. But you can sometimes reframe (tactfully!) any negative comments made by other adults.

> Jamil's so untidy–not like his sister!

> Jamil's learning to put things away and he's doing really well. He did a great job of sorting my tools yesterday.

Luckily, you will have more influence than the doom-mongers!

Making mistakes and sticking at it

Being afraid of getting things wrong can be a real barrier to learning – and it can stop us from doing things that we really want to do.

- As a family, try to treat mistakes as an opportunity to learn.

- When your child makes a mistake, simply talk to her about what went wrong, and encourage her to think about what she needs to do next time. Support her as she has another go.

- Share your own mistakes and what you've learned from them – where appropriate. When your child sees that you are OK with making mistakes, she will learn to have the same attitude.

- Encourage your child to keep going – even when the going gets tough.
  Children who have not learned to persevere and who give up easily will find it harder to achieve things in life.

- Persevere at things yourself. When your child sees you do this, she will learn to do the same.

Essential skills for life in the 21st century

We now live in a world where the rate of change is accelerating. Many things that were taken for granted are no longer certain. Jobs, for example, are changing rapidly. The days of a 'job for life' are long gone, and people often have to switch careers, possibly more than once.

In this sort of world, it is life skills that will make all the difference. People with these skills will have resilience to cope when things don't turn out as expected. They will not be fazed by problems, but will have the resources to find solutions. They will not be put off by apparent failure, and will persevere until they succeed.

Most importantly, perhaps, a person with life skills will be able to make the sort of relationships that give a sense of identity and belonging – and that's what will really bring happiness.

You may find that as you try some of these things with your child, it has a positive effect on you, too!

When it comes to life skills, we're all learning all the time.

QUICK CHECK

✓ Being happy and fulfilled comes from lots of things, not just academic success.

✓ Your child is more likely to fulfil her potential in learning and in life if she has developed 'life skills'.

✓ Life skills can be learned and improved at any age – but before the age of six is an especially good time.

✓ Becoming aware of our own attitudes and behaviour is an important step in helping our children.

✓ A positive attitude to mistakes is vital for success in learning and in life.

Everybody's Different

Did you know...

? Intelligence is not something fixed at birth?

? Intelligence takes many forms?

? From an early age, boys and girls tend to have different strengths?

It's not how smart you are, but how you are smart. *Howard Gardner*

WHAT ARE YOUR STRENGTHS?

Take a moment to imagine yourself in each of these situations. What if you had to:

- ★ write and give a speech
- ★ read a book in order to find out about something important to you
- ★ learn how to use a new high-tech gadget – like a phone or DVD player
- ★ work out your personal or family finances
- ☆ design a room and choose new decor
- ☆ find and follow a route on a map
- ★ take part in a half-marathon
- ★ join in with everyone on the dance floor
- ★ compile a selection of music for a party
- ★ sing a song or play an instrument
- ☆ resolve an argument between two friends or work colleagues
- ☆ organize an outing for a group of people
- ★ go on a long country walk
- ★ look after friends' animals and plants while they're away
- ★ take part in a group discussion about whether it's ever right to lie
- ★ complete a quiz to do with personality!?

What do you feel as you imagine yourself in each situation? Which make you feel interested or excited? Which make you feel anxious or apprehensive?

As adults we have individual strengths and preferences, and knowing what these are is part of knowing ourselves and being comfortable with who we are. It can also help us to be aware of other people's strengths and preferences – including those of our children.

Each pair of questions (shown by the coloured stars) above relates to one of the areas of intelligence on pages 29–30. So your answers to these may help you work out your own 'multiple intelligence profile'.

Everybody is different

All 3–5 year olds have a lot in common (see Chapter 1), but already their individual differences are becoming clear. You will almost certainly be aware of:

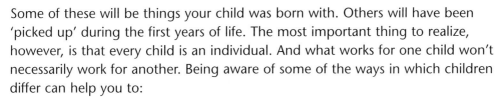

- your child's personality – for example, he might be boisterous or quiet, sociable or shy;
- his particular interests and preferences;
- things which he seems able to do especially well – perhaps better than most other children of his age;
- things which he finds difficult.

Some of these will be things your child was born with. Others will have been 'picked up' during the first years of life. The most important thing to realize, however, is that every child is an individual. And what works for one child won't necessarily work for another. Being aware of some of the ways in which children differ can help you to:

- understand your own child better;
- help him in the ways that suit him;
- help him develop his strengths;
- help him improve at things he finds more difficult.

PAUSE FOR THOUGHT: No comparison

Einstein didn't speak until he was four years old. So try not to compare your child's progress with that of his friends or brothers and sisters. All children develop differently, and doing things early is not necessarily an indication of super-intelligence. Some children who show early signs of ability in a particular area are 'overtaken' by others later on.

But in any case, it is not a race. The important thing is to give your child the encouragement and support he needs to learn when he is ready. With the right support, all children can be successful.

Ways of being intelligent

Until fairly recently, people tended to think of intelligence as a single characteristic, rather like height or shoe size. They thought that, like height or shoe size, it was something you could measure – which they did, using IQ tests. One problem with this was that someone may be good at art, or music or sport, but this would not be measured by IQ tests. (In fact, some people say that the only thing really measured by IQ tests is … the ability to do IQ tests!)

Nowadays, we appreciate that 'intelligence' can take many forms, and that people have strengths in different areas. Various psychologists have come up with theories to describe the different sorts of intelligence or ability. On the next two pages, you'll find eight descriptions of children with different abilities, based on one of these theories: Howard Gardner's **multiple intelligences**.

See if you recognize your child – and perhaps yourself and other members of your family – in any of them. Many people are strong in more than one area.

Having an idea of your child's strengths can help in a number of ways:

- You can help him develop his strengths. As he becomes really good at something, this will boost his confidence and self-esteem – which in turn will give him confidence to develop in his weaker areas as well.

- People are always happier when they are doing something in a way that plays to their strengths. So using a strength can be a good way for your child to learn something.

- You can be aware of where he needs extra support and encouragement. It's important for children to develop their skills and abilities in all areas, including the ones where they are weaker.

You may have a clear picture of your child's preferences and abilities, but if not, don't worry! The really important thing at this stage is to offer him a wide variety of experiences so he can find his strengths. And developing all the different types of intelligence will help your child to learn more easily as well as become a well-rounded individual.

Your child may:

- speak well and be talkative;
- have 'a feel for words';
- experiment with rhymes and the sounds of words;
- enjoy stories and show great interest in books.

(linguistic intelligence)

Your child may:

- notice patterns and creates patterns in his play;
- like sorting things into categories;
- be interested in problems.

(logical–mathematical intelligence)

Your child may:

- love drawing, copying, painting and making models;
- be good at jigsaw puzzles and memory games;
- remember journeys and recognize landmarks.

(visual–spatial intelligence)

Your child may:

- have good co-ordination and enjoy physical activity;
- use his hands well and like using tools;
- be a good dancer, actor or mimic.

(bodily–kinesthetic intelligence)

Your child may:

- enjoy listening to music;
- love to sing, chant, rap and make up songs;
- have an ear for a tune and a good sense of rhythm.

(musical intelligence)

Your child may:

- enjoy playing with others;
- notice and show sympathy if others are upset;
- be good at seeing other people's point of view.

(interpersonal intelligence)

Your child may:

- tend to think deeply about things;
- be able to see situations surprisingly clearly;
- be good at talking about his own thoughts and feelings;
- be very honest – often coming out with the very thing you don't want at the most inappropriate moment.

(intrapersonal intelligence)

Your child may:

- love plants and animals, enjoy identifying them and finding out about them;
- enjoy being outdoors;
- enjoy looking after pets or plants.

(naturalistic intelligence)

Boys and girls

If you happen to have one of each, you may have noticed some differences. (Apart from the obvious.) Differences between girls and boys probably arise because of subtle differences in male and female brains and from the effects of the male hormone, testosterone, on the development of boys.

It is generally agreed that young girls **tend** to:

- have a larger vocabulary and speak more fluently than boys of similar age;
- find it easier to listen and to concentrate.

Boys, on the other hand, **tend** to:

- be better at activities requiring spatial awareness, such as model making and puzzles;
- have boundless energy for physical play, action and adventure.

Many young boys find it extremely difficult to meet the demands of school because the activities tend to be geared towards the preferences of girls. It's not that boys are any less able than girls, but that they often have different strengths and prefer different learning styles. And many develop their language and literacy skills at a slightly later stage.

These are big generalizations: there will be obvious exceptions to the rule as well as wide variation between girls and between boys. Nevertheless, it may be helpful to be aware of possible differences – especially if you have a son who seems unable to listen and doesn't sit still for a minute.
If this is the case, these ideas may help:

- Give your son one task at a time. There is growing evidence to show that girls really do find it easier to multi-task than boys.
- Make your instructions clear and precise.
- In conversations with your son, be patient and try not to hurry him.
- Share lots of books with him, and tune into his interests. Many boys prefer information books to stories.

- Provide plenty of opportunity for exercise and rough-and-tumble play.
- Help him to see the importance of thinking before acting. Talk with him about alternative ways of solving problems – without hitting or hurting.

- Provide opportunities to take things apart and join things together. This will help him to develop the fine motor skills necessary for writing.
- Help him to develop manipulative skills through using tools, cooking utensils, brushes, scissors, and so on.

As you may realize, these are all very good things to do with young children of either sex!

But I've noticed ...

As we've tried to show in this chapter, there's a wide range of ability and rate of development in 3–5 year olds – and that's quite normal. However, if you have a hunch that your child is having unusual difficulty with talking, learning or behaviour, or if there's some aspect of his physical development that is giving you concern, then do talk to someone. If your child is at school or a pre-school setting, then have a word with the staff. Or you could go to your family doctor. If your child does have a special educational need, the sooner it is identified, the sooner he can be given appropriate help and support.

QUICK CHECK

✓ There are lots of different ways in which people can be intelligent.

✓ Recognizing and developing a child's strengths will increase competence and confidence.

✓ Developing all the different types of intelligence can help children to learn more easily.

✓ Boys and girls may have different strengths and learning styles.

Healthy Body, Healthy Mind

Did you know...

? What your child eats now will affect her health in later life?

? Physical exercise is important for brain development?

? Getting enough sleep is vital for learning?

> **The brain is very sensitive to what's happening in the body.** *Professor Susan Greenfield*

GOOD FOOD AND EXERCISE?

Take a moment to think back to when you were a child.

★ What can you remember about mealtimes? Did your family eat together? What were family mealtimes like?

★ What sort of things did you enjoy eating?

★ What sort of things did you dislike eating?

★ Were you made to eat certain things – or to have a clean plate?

★ What sweets and snacks were you allowed?

★ What were bedtimes like? Did you have a regular bedtime?

★ In what ways were you physically active? Did you walk to school, play in the park, or play outside with your friends?

Do you think your childhood experiences have influenced what you eat today and the amount of exercise and sleep you have?

What would the answers to these questions be for your child? In what ways are her diet, exercise and bedtimes the same as yours as a child, and in what ways are they different?

Bodies and brains

People used to see thinking and learning as brain activity that had little to do with the rest of the body. But research is revealing that the mind and the body are more closely linked than we ever imagined:

- **Exercise** keeps both body and brain healthy. Lack of physical exercise in the early years can inhibit brain development and lead to learning difficulties.
- **A good diet** helps our brains to function well.
- **Sleep** is vital for all sorts of brain functions, including learning. While we sleep, the brain processes learning that has taken place during the day and transfers it into long-term memory.

So making sure your child eats well, sleeps well and has plenty of exercise will help her stay healthy. It will also help her brain to develop and function well.

As we take care of children's physical needs, we are also teaching them how to care for themselves. The most effective way to do this is to set a good example. If your child sees that you think it's important to take care of your body, she will be more likely to do the same.

Eating

The fact that many young children are not eating healthily has become a matter of public concern. In the UK, the United States and other countries there are increasing numbers of obese children who are very likely to become obese adults – with all the associated health risks.

Nutritionists say that eating habits are established in childhood. So what your child is eating now is laying the foundations for her future health and wellbeing. How can you establish a pattern of healthy eating? To start with, it's helpful to think of all foods as having some value, rather than as 'good' or 'bad' foods. So 'healthy eating' doesn't mean a diet consisting of lettuce and lentils. It's about making sure your child gets a balance of different foods. W

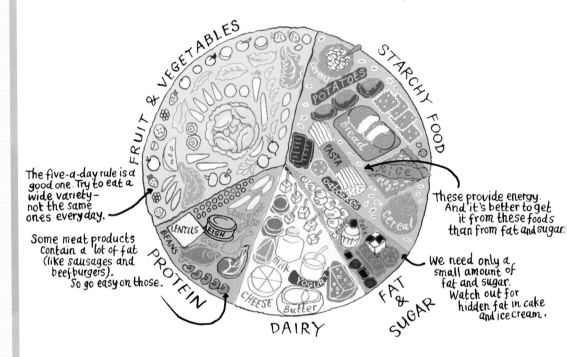

The five-a-day rule is a good one. Try to eat a wide variety – not the same ones everyday.

Some meat products contain a lot of fat (like sausages and beefburgers). So go easy on those.

These provide energy. And it's better to get it from these foods than from fat and sugar.

We need only a small amount of fat and sugar. Watch out for hidden fat in cake and ice cream.

Ready meals and other convenience foods tend to have a lot of fat, sugar and salt and fewer of the nutrients your body and brain needs. Be suspicious of long lists of ingredients. So frozen vegetables – fine; frozen lasagne – probably not.

ip for better behaviour and improved concentration

Enjoy a good breakfast! If you're struggling just to get everyone up, dressed and out in the morning, it's tempting to skip it. But many studies have shown that children who eat a good breakfast tend to do better at school, have better concentration and behaviour and are less hyperactive.

All together now!

For all sorts of reasons, very few families now sit round the table to eat meals together. A recent study in the UK found 20 per cent of families never do it and most of those who do tend to have the TV on as well.

But research has shown that family meals are a really good thing for children of all ages because:

- they tend to be healthier – everyone sits down to a planned meal, rather than snacking or grazing individually around the kitchen;
- children learn healthy eating, table manners and social skills from the adults;
- they help to provide much-needed routine for young children;
- they're an opportunity for everyone to talk about what's happened in their day and to plan future activities together.

Please would you pass the broccoli, Tom?

What did you do today, Mum?

So if you can arrange to eat together, even if it's only two or three times a week, everyone will benefit.

ip for when your child won't eat something

If your child doesn't like something, don't give up. Research shows that children may need to try a new food up to ten times before they like it. Each time you offer it, tell her that she need only eat a little bit – and the chances are that sooner or later she'll ask for more!

I'm hungry!

There is good evidence that children really do know when they need food and when they don't. So if you're going to establish healthy eating habits, it's important you don't inadvertently teach your child to ignore what her body is telling her. When your child says 'I'm hungry', feed her. When she says 'I'm full', don't force her to 'eat up'.

But I'm hungry NOW!

Dinner will be in half an hour. If you're hungry, would you like this carrot?

If she says she's hungry before a mealtime, then offer a nutritious snack such as fruit or raw vegetables. Sometimes children say they are hungry when really they are just bored. If she refuses your offer and demands a chocolate bar, then she probably isn't really hungry and will be just fine waiting until the meal.

I'm not hungry!

If your child won't eat at mealtimes, the number one rule is: don't get stressed. Remember, most children know when they need food, so your child is unlikely to starve herself. Of course, don't allow her to leave the table and then stock up on things like chocolate bars, cookies, bags of salty snacks, or even sugary drinks.

So what about the salty snacks and chocolate bars?

It's unrealistic to expect that we or our children should not eat any of these foods. The odd treat is fine. Just make sure that a sweet or savoury treat is just one of many foods offered through the day. And explain that these things are bad for us when we eat too many of them.

Tips for eating for better behaviour

- Be wary of sugary drinks and processed snacks – as well as having a lot of calories without any other nutrition, many have additives that can make children hyperactive.
- Don't use food as a reward or a bribe – it will teach your child to eat for comfort.

Exercise

Children today are less physically active than ever before. This is a problem because, as we all know, physical activity helps to keep us healthy and prevents us becoming overweight. More surprisingly, perhaps, research is showing that:

- physical activity appears to boost academic performance;
- movement is essential for brain development and learning.

It turns out that lots of things young children do instinctively are actually important for brain development:

Crawling and balancing
Moving alternate arms and legs helps to make connections between the two sides of the brain – connections which are vital for literacy later on.

Hanging upside down
Seeing how the world looks the other way up helps when it comes to seeing the difference between letters like **b** and **d**.

Spinning
Whirling around makes the ear fluid move rapidly inside the ear. This in turn helps grow new cells in a part of the brain that develops the 'muscle memory' needed for reading and writing.

All of these are things that most young children do anyway – given half a chance. So you don't have to send your three year old off to the gym. All the exercise she needs can happen in the course of everyday life...

Out and about

- Incorporate physical activity into your daily routine where you can – use stairs instead of the escalator; walk to the shops instead of taking the car.

- Play on the swings, climbing frames and other equipment at the local playground.

- Play chasing games and ball games – or invent different types of races.

- Set up an obstacle course, using whatever is available. Involving her in constructing the obstacles develops creative and imaginative thinking.

over

THROUGH

ACROSS

UNDER

through the tunnel and under the low bridge

> Our children are increasingly battery-raised – cooped up in their homes, living virtual lives, or in the car, being transported from club to class to club – rather than enjoying the free-range existence they could expect even twenty-five years ago. *Sue Palmer*

ACTIVITY: Bottle bowling

Fill some large plastic bottles with water and set them up as skittles. Use some heavy balls to see how many each of you can knock down. Have a pencil and paper handy for keeping the score. On a warm summer's day, try playing this game with sponges soaked in a bucket of water.

Aiming at the skittles will develop your child's hand–eye co-ordination, which is important for writing. Throwing the balls develops strength and physical dexterity. Counting the number of bottles knocked down will also develop number skills.

Indoors

- Put on some music – and dance!

- Imitate animal movements: walk like a penguin, hop like a frog and so on.

- Sing action songs (with the actions, of course!)

- Sit on the ground and let your child step over your legs. Make a bridge with your body and let him crawl under.

And, most importantly, have fun!

Screen time

One reason children today are less active is the amount of time they spend sitting in front of a computer or television.

Children can get a lot from TV and computers, but it's best to limit the amount of time your child spends in front of a screen. No more than an hour a day is enough for 3–5 year olds (see page 70).

Sleep

Sleep is vital. It's just as important for your child's development as healthy eating and exercise, and 3–5 year olds need anything from 11 to 13 hours a night. Lack of sleep affects children's behaviour as well as their ability to think and learn. In the long term, it can actually hinder the development of a child's brain.

W Sleep experts all say that young children benefit from going to bed at a regular time and having a familiar bedtime routine.

Bath time

Teeth

Story

Goodnight and lights out

Being firm

Sleep!

QUICK CHECK

✓ Healthy children are happier and learn more effectively.
✓ If you have a healthy lifestyle, your child will copy.
✓ A balanced diet and plenty of exercise are vital for young bodies and brains.
✓ 3–5 year olds need 11–13 hours' sleep.

Did you know that researchers estimate that two thirds of young children in the UK do not get enough sleep?

Let's Play!

5

Did you know...

? Play is one of the most important ways young children learn?

? Play is a vital preparation for reading and writing?

? The best play things don't cost a lot of money?

"Play is like a reservoir full of water. The deeper the reservoir, the more water can be stored in it and used in times of drought. The benefits of childhood play are of lasting impact during adult life, both through good and bad times. *Tina Bruce* **"**

WHAT DID YOU PLAY?

Take a moment to think about the things you liked to do when you were very young. Did you enjoy:

- ★ playing with dirt, mud, soil or sand
- ★ climbing things
- ★ making dens
- ★ pretending to be a character from a story or film
- ★ playing in puddles
- ★ playing ball games
- ★ singing and making up songs
- ★ dancing to music
- ★ having a teddy bears' picnic or a dolls' tea party
- ★ putting 'stuff' in water and mixing it all up
- ★ arranging play people in a house or animals in a farm
- ★ painting, drawing, cutting and gluing
- ★ dressing up
- ★ taking things apart and putting them together again
- ★ making up stories and plays
- ★ playing hide-and-seek and frightening people
- ★ mashing up petals in water to make 'perfume'
- ★ digging big holes
- ★ rough and tumble play with brothers, sisters, cousins or friends?

Are there any other activities you would add to the list?

Which of these things did you enjoy most?

Do you know which your child enjoys?

Which has he had the opportunity to try?

Play is vital

Play is not simply a way of keeping small children amused. It's the way they learn. When your child is playing, he is developing:

- physical skills – including the ability to manipulate objects
- creativity and imagination
- language
- mathematical skills
- knowledge and understanding of the world
- concentration
- perseverance
- independence
- resilience
- confidence
- the ability to solve problems
- the ability to adapt things and be flexible
- skills for resolving conflicts
- understanding of how one thing can symbolize another – vital for literacy.

And all of this will happen while he is having fun and enjoying himself.

AUSE FOR THOUGHT:

Watch your child when he is really enjoying himself playing. Then look at the list and decide which things you see happening. You might be surprised at what's going on before your very eyes!

You may notice that as your child gets older, there are opportunities to do all sorts of exciting activities. It's easy to feel that unless your child is learning gym, swimming, judo and violin, then he might be missing out. These more formal activities do have something to offer – learning special skills can be stimulating and boost confidence. But remember that, most of all, children of this age need time for their own free play.

Things to play with

You do not have to spend a lot of money on toys for your child to play with. In fact, some of the best things for play are quite inexpensive – or free. Here are some ideas. Many items could be used in more than one type of activity: when your child is playing with containers and a sink full of water, it's very likely he'll be developing his vocabulary and imagination along with his ideas about the how the world works.

use an old comb to make patterns when the paint is wet

no paint to mix on

wear an old shirt

sponging background

finger paints

things to print with

cork hands

leaves

sponge

bottle tops

scissors

old birthday cards

glue

feathers

beads

buttons

sequins

yarn

cotton wool

coloured paper

old magazines and brochures

Model making

use rolling pins on the play dough

monster

Pipecleaners for arms and legs

toilet roll snake-thread toilet rolls onto string

cut up old boxes to use - egg boxes too

cardboard head

masking tape

sellotape

keep rubber bands

drinking straws

paper cups

wire coat hangers

and string and rope

Sorting and matching

- shells
- pebbles
- egg boxes
- pasta shapes
- beads
- jars
- old tins

Water

- watering can
- colander
- toy boat
- corks
- straws
- ping pong balls
- plastic bottles
- funnel
- sponge
- plastic jugs

Dressing up

- hats
- bags
- scarves
- jewellery
- old clothes
- ribbons
- shoes
- hairbands
- belts

Making a den

old sheets or curtains pegged onto chairs

boxes and cushions inside for furniture

> **Play is a serious business.**
> *David Attenborough*

47

Playing with your child

Sometimes your child will be quite happy playing by himself – he'll appear to be 'lost in his own world' – and that's great. There will also be times when he'll like having you join in. And sometimes he may need your encouragement to get started on a new play activity.

I'm building a tower and I'm using blue and yellow bricks and I think I might use some of these green ones.

Watch your child to see how he is using the things he is playing with, then copy what he is doing. As you copy, describe what you are doing. Talk to yourself, rather than to him.

If your child is so deeply engrossed that he takes no notice, then just creep away quietly. He may even tell you to go away! Don't be offended. He is just following an important thread of thinking. But he may respond, and then you are accepted into the play.

Don't use the green, these purple ones are better.

That looks interesting. What are you building there?

It's a garage for the cars.

Once you are a part of the play, you have an opportunity to extend your child's thinking. Talk with him about his play. Ask questions about what he is doing, and listen carefully to what he has to say.

Make suggestions.
(But be prepared to
have them rejected!)

Offer additional materials
that will enable him to
extend his play. Be excited
about what he is playing.

Playing with your child
will greatly benefit his
learning. And if you really
listen to him, it can give
you a valuable insight into
how his mind is working.

ip for when you can't play right now

Playing with your child is important. But don't feel guilty if you can't
supply attention on demand all the time. It is also important for him to
learn that he will sometimes have to wait for what he wants. Gently
explain that although you would really like to play with him, you cannot do
it right now. Tell him the reason why you can't play at that moment, and
reassure him that you will as soon as you are able. Make sure you keep
your promise so he learns that his waiting will be rewarded.

ips for organising play stuff

Use plastic containers or baskets to store play materials. Write labels to show what's inside each box. This will help your child to understand how we use writing to help organize our lives.

You could also take photos of the box contents, then put a photo on each box with a written label underneath.

Batteries not included

Technology is part of children's world, and it has also become part of their play. Electronic toys can seem very attractive to young children. Often, they provide a lot of excitement at first – only for the child to lose interest.

The reason is that most electronic toys leave nothing to the imagination and so do not provide the same possibilities for play as more traditional ones.

Children's imagination is more powerful than a set of batteries

That's not to say all electronic toys are poor value. Hours of fun can be had from things like:

a child's cassette player   a microphone   an electronic keyboard

Again, again!

When a game or activity is over – and just when you're more than ready to give it a rest – your child may well be shouting 'Again!' All young children do this. It's because they are exploring ideas. So even if it feels rather tedious, let him do it again if possible.

Playing with others

Young children – even as small babies – enjoy the company of others their own age. And from around the age of three, friends become increasingly important. Try to provide plenty of opportunities for your child to play with others.

When young children play together, there are inevitably squabbles as they learn the skills of collaboration and co-operation. However, you can take steps to avoid unnecessary conflict. So if your child has a friend round to play, put away any treasured items, such as special teddies. And provide toys where there is plenty of the same thing, such as building bricks or play dough.

- Talk about the importance of sharing, and help him to practise taking turns.
- Help him to understand that people who work well with others are able to achieve more than people who do not.
- When a squabble does break out, don't rush in straight away but encourage them to sort it out for themselves. If after a while there's no sign of that happening, then you'll have to enter the fray. (See resolving conflicts on page 20.)

Play and gender

Don't limit your child's play by giving him – or her – only things you think are 'for boys' – or 'for girls'. Boys benefit from playing with dolls just as girls benefit from playing with toy cars and construction kits.

Play and computers

Young children can benefit from computer games and activities. As well as learning new things, using the mouse and keyboard develops motor skills and co-ordination. Using the computer should be just one of lots of different activities.

- For pre-school children, a short session of about 15 minutes three or four times a week is probably enough.
- Don't let your child sit too close to the screen.
- **W** Look for computer programs that require children to think and to solve problems or make decisions, or that encourage creativity – such as painting programs.
- Never let your child use a computer program or website that you haven't personally checked out.

QUICK CHECK

✓ Play is vital for children's development.

✓ Many of the best materials for play are inexpensive or free.

✓ Children need experience of playing alone, playing with an adult, and playing with other children.

✓ Children play with ideas as well as with things.

Did you know that lack of energetic, physical activity can hinder a child's development and lead to frustration and difficult behaviour?

Wonderful World!

6

Did you know...

? Children explore the world using all their senses?

? You don't need any special equipment to help your child be a scientist?

? It doesn't matter if you don't know all the answers to all those questions!

> Although the minutiae of domestic life may be commonplace for adults, it's still new and original for young children, and seeing it through a child's eyes allows adults to rediscover all the small wonders forgotten in our usual busyness. *Sue Palmer*

WHAT FASCINATED YOU?

Take a moment to think back to when you were a child. Can you remember times when you were completely absorbed in something?
Was it:

- ★ a muddy puddle
- ★ slugs and snails
- ★ rockpools at the seaside
- ★ the hosepipe in the garden
- ★ a pile of logs
- ★ the insides of a clock or radio
- ★ the flames in a fire or on a candle
- ★ clouds moving across the sky
- ★ bubbles in the bath
- ★ the contents of a drawer or cupboard
- ★ melting ice
- ★ a stream
- ★ sand on the beach
- ★ a big machine, like a tractor
- ★ … or something else?

What things fascinated you as a child?

What was it like to be completely absorbed in something?

Can you see any connection between those things and the things you are interested in now?

What fascinates your own child?

The big project

From the moment she was born, your child has been engaged in a big project: she's been busy figuring out how the world works and trying to make sense of it all. By the age of three, the investigation is in full swing – which is why children of this age often produce an endless stream of questions. In fact, although you may not have realized it, she probably has you working as her No 1 assistant in her investigation.

So how can you help your child as she learns about the world? The most valuable thing you can do is make time for conversation. Simply talk to your child about things around her and about what she's doing. If you listen carefully, you'll get some useful insight into what she's thinking.

Why don't worms have legs?

Because their bodies are shaped so they can move through the soil easily.

Why do they go through the soil?

Because that's where they find their food.

I don't eat soil. What sort of food is in the soil?

Hmm... I'm not sure. Shall we see if we can find a book that will tell us?

PAUSE FOR THOUGHT: With the eyes of a child

If you have visited another country, try to recall what it felt like to be in a place where things like food, buildings and social customs were different – and you didn't understand everything that was going on.

Using the senses

Young children explore the world using all their senses – seeing, hearing, touching, tasting and smelling. And of course, they don't know that you're not supposed to taste the crayons, feel the yogurt and smell the guinea pig! But by using the all their senses, they are gathering important information. So:

- Whenever possible, answer her questions by showing rather than telling. Let her look, feel, hear – and generally try things for herself.
- When appropriate, encourage her to look, hear, touch, taste and smell.

Research suggests that the more senses that are involved in an experience, the better the learning is remembered.

Asking questions

Asking a question is a good way to start a conversation. And the key is to go for quality rather than quantity.

● Ask questions that will invite thought and stimulate imagination.

For example:

● Ask questions that will invite thought and stimulate the imagination.

● Allow your child time to think.

● Listen carefully to what she says before you reply. If what she says seems wrong or silly, don't dismiss it as wrong or silly. Instead, you might ask another, different question to find out more about what she's thinking.

Answering questions

When your child asks questions, take them seriously. And they can be worth listening to – young children do ask the most interesting questions!

Why is the sky blue?

How do the pictures get into the TV?

Why don't the eggs in the box hatch?

How do we know Tibby is a girl?

Try to give an answer your child can understand. And always use the correct words. They are no more difficult, and children like knowing and being able to use them. If you don't know the answer, say so. Then talk about how you might find out together.

Where does the wind come from?

Hmm, that's a good question! I don't think I know the answer to that. We could look it up on the internet, or go to the library.

Uncle Bill knows about the weather, we could ask him.

That's a good idea! We'll phone him tonight and see if he can help us.

Sometimes, however, your child may just want a straight answer so she can get on with whatever she is doing.

Big and awkward

At this age, children often ask 'big' questions, to which there are no easy answers. It's best just to be as honest as you can – without causing your child undue concern.

Where did Grandpa go when he died?

They can also ask awkward questions. Bear in mind, though, that the question is only awkward to you because you know the answer!

But how did the baby get into your tummy?

Finding out about the world

W Encourage your child's natural curiosity about the world. There are lots of opportunities for investigation and discussion at home and places nearby.

In the kitchen ...

try growing leftover pips and seeds and carrot tops

Cut open fruits and vegetables and look inside

make ice cubes and watch them melt

have fun with flour or squidge some dough

look at labels to see where food comes from

measure count weigh estimate

how much water can a sponge hold?

experiment with a siphon

sink a bottle for lots of bubbles

what floats?

what sinks?

In the bathroom ...

In the garden ...

investigate tools

keep an eye on the weather

grow some vegetables

go on a mini-beast safari

what's in a spadeful of soil?

what's new? what's old?

spot the shapes

notice the numbers

talk about places and routes

what makes things go?

In the street ...

Did you know that research has shown that contact with natural environment has a calming effect on children?

ACTIVITY: Treasure Hunt

Make a list of all the things you are going to hunt for. What you include will depend partly on where you're going to hunt – park, garden, seaside and so on. Making the list will help your child learn about writing and how it is used.

a stone
a flower
a leaf
a stick
something red
something prickly
a coin
something made
of plastic
something soft
something smooth

Once you have made your list, time how long it takes to find everything. (This will develop her sense of time.)

Talk about all the 'treasure' you find. Sort the items – which will help her to develop classification skills. Count the numbers of each type.

ACTIVITY: Fun things to do with a camera

If you have a digital camera, take some photos of something that's changing over a period of time. For example: seeds growing, baby animals growing, a garden in the different seasons.

Looking at the sequence of photos will help your child develop a sense of time. You could print the photos and make them into a zigzag book.

Counting and sorting

From the age of three, children are beginning to understand numbers, patterns, shape and measurement. These are all foundations for the maths skills that she'll learn later on. You can help your child just by showing her the maths that you use in everyday life – whether it's checking the number of the TV channel you want to watch, counting out knives and forks to lay the table, or deciding who gets the *biggest* slice of cake!

matching and finding pairs

pointing out numbers *three !*

five little speckled frogs

singing counting rhymes and songs

that's the biggest!

comparing

four... five

counting

first shoe

talking about order

triangles today!

recognizing and naming shapes

ACTIVITY: Button box

Make a collection of buttons in a box or tin. Tip the buttons out onto a tray or other suitable surface and watch what your child does with them. She will probably begin to sort, match, count, compare and make patterns. Talk with your child about what she is doing and encourage her to think about where the different sorts of buttons might have come from. If there are buttons from some of her old clothes, remembering the clothes and when she wore them will help develop her sense of time.

You can also do this activity with collections of pebbles, shells or coins.

It's an electronic world

Your child was born into a digital, high-tech world – very different from the one you were born into. Remember that your child has not known a world without computers, DVDs and phones you take around with you.

Children really like exploring and using technology, and it's important they understand how it works and how it can help. They need to be shown how to use it safely, correctly – and wisely.

Tips for using technology with children

- **Teach your child to use electronic equipment**. Show her how to use the television, CD player and video or DVD player correctly. Again, use the correct words: *load*, *eject*, *click*, and so on.

- **Notice technology** when you're out and about – look at traffic lights, pedestrian crossings and barcode scanners. Talk about what each is used for and how it helps.

- **Let her use appropriate programs and websites**. (See page 52.) Let her watch you using the computer, and explain what you are using it for.

- **Keep computers in family space**. You wouldn't leave your child in a room with an unknown adult, but if you leave your child alone with a computer or TV you may be leaving her with 'the stranger on the screen'.

- **Keep it real**. Young children need plenty of real-life experience, so make sure that computers and other electronic gadgetry are not your child's main source of amusement.

QUICK CHECK

✓ Ask questions that will get your child thinking.
✓ Give your child opportunities to investigate the world around her.
✓ Look out for opportunities to use 'everyday' maths together.
✓ Help her to explore technology and learn how to use it properly.

Wonderful Words!

Did you know...

? Children are 'hard-wired' to acquire language – it's as natural as learning to walk?

? That between the ages of three and four, a child's vocabulary increases from 1,000 words to about 5,000 words, on average?

? That one of the best ways to boost your child's chances of success in reading and writing is simply to talk to him?

"" Early literacy thrives when it is nourished on a rich diet of gossip, anecdotes, reminiscences and storytelling. *Marian Whitehead* ""

WHAT STORIES, RHYMES AND SONGS DID YOU ENJOY?

Take a moment to think back to when you were a young child.

Can you remember:

- ⋆ stories that you heard
- ⋆ nursery rhymes you learned
- ⋆ songs you sang
- ⋆ picture books that you enjoyed
- ⋆ favourite children's TV programmes
- ⋆ learning to read and write? (Adults who have no memories of this usually found the process easy; adults who remember often found it more difficult.)

What was your early experience of books and reading like? Was it a source of pleasure or anxiety?

How might your feelings affect the experience you provide for your own child?

Of the books, rhymes and songs you remember, are there any that your own child now enjoys?

If possible, discuss your answers with your partner or with a friend.

Literacy – being able to read and write – is the foundation of school learning and a vital set of skills for success in life. Most children start reading and writing during their first year at school. But the learning that leads up to this amazing achievement has been going on since birth.

There's a lot you can do to help prepare your child for reading and writing. One of the best things is sharing books and stories together. As well as increasing awareness of language and print, stories develop your child's understanding of how the world works.

Sharing books

Build up a varied collection of good quality picture books to share with your child. (See page 91 for some suggestions.) And of course you can visit the library for regular fresh supplies. When you're having a book time with your child:

Read with expression.

Talk about the pictures. Ask him to tell you about them.

Encourage your child to join in - especially when there are repeated words or phrases.

Choose a book you like - if you're enjoying it, your child probably will too.

Look at the front cover and the title. If it's a new book, you might discuss what you both think it's going to be about.

Point to the words as you read them.

Talk about the story. Ask him to guess what happens next.

- Encourage your child to 'read' the book – to you or to visitors. If he doesn't use the exact words or even tells the story differently, that's fine.
- If your child obviously doesn't like a particular book, then leave it and try again in a few months' time. Meanwhile, try some different ones.
- Be willing to read the same book again and again if your child wants it. The repetition will be helping him to learn.

Read little and often. And most of all, have fun! By doing this, you will be helping your child to learn how books work. He will see:

that books have a front...

...and a back

how to hold a book the right way up

how to turn the pages correctly

that text goes from left to right and top to bottom (when reading English)

how to tell a story through the pictures

that text has meaning

You may find your child beginning to recognize letters (especially ones in his own name) and then words. Some children learn to read 'naturally', through adults sharing books with them. If you share books regularly with your child, it's quite possible that he will become one of these 'natural' readers.

ACTIVITY: Make your own book

A book that your child will definitely find interesting is one made especially for him – about him and things in his life. There are all sorts of possibilities: here are just a couple of ideas.

- Use a digital camera to take photos of a day out or a special occasion. On the computer, import the pictures into a word-processing or publishing program. Invite your child to 'tell the story' for you to type under the pictures. Then print out the pages of your book.

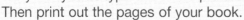

- Make your own alphabet, number or colour book – use pictures cut from magazines, or photos of things in your house, or a mixture of both.

Listening

PAUSE FOR THOUGHT: Can they hear us?

We live in a noisy world filled with TV, DVDs and downloaded music – but do we really listen? It's probably harder for our children to listen: research has shown that children who have constant background noise such as a TV find it harder to pick out the sound of their mother's voice.

Listening underpins all learning, and the first skills children have to acquire are the ability to pick out a single sound from background noise, and to distinguish between different sounds. Help your child by listening for the sounds you can hear in different places – at home, in the park, on a walk.

ACTIVITY: Sound games

Collect a variety of objects that make a noise, for example a timer, some keys, some spoons, a jar of rice, a squeaky toy. Explore the objects with your child, encouraging him to listen carefully to the sound that each one makes. Put a blindfold on him (or get him to face the other way) then make a sound with one of the objects. See if he can say which object made the noise. Then swap roles with your child. When you have played a few times, try using items that sound similar, for more of a challenge.

Simply having conversations with your child is helping him to tune into language and preparing him for reading.

- When your child is speaking, pay him full attention and show you are listening.
- Encourage him to take turns in conversation, and show appreciation when he listens without interrupting.
- Try not to correct errors in his speech, as it will destroy his confidence. You may be able to rephrase what he has said in your reply, for example:

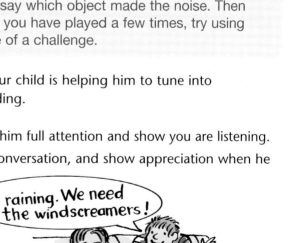

It's raining. We need the windscreamers!

Yes, you're right, I'll switch the windscreen wipers on.

Rhymes and songs

Enjoy lots of rhymes and songs together. This might not seem as if it has much to do with reading and writing, but it helps to develop:

A sense of rhyme – if a child can hear when words contain the same sound, he will later be able to make the link between words that sound the same and words with the same spelling pattern – which helps with learning to read.

A sense of beat – this underlies our ability to pick up the patterns of sound in language. Research has shown that young children who can feel and maintain a steady beat are more likely to be successful in school. A sense of rhythm is also important for all sorts of other activities, from dancing to hammering in a nail.

Memory – readers have to be able to remember the words they have just read so they can make sense of whatever they are reading.

There are lots of ways to have fun with rhymes and songs:

- **Sing songs and nursery rhymes**. Don't worry about the quality of your own voice – your child won't mind if it lacks star quality. Tapes or CDs can help, and are great for car journeys. It's worth taking care over your choice – if you don't want to be driven mad by the sound of synthesized songs that all sound the same. See page 92 for some worth trying. When your child knows a rhyme well, try pausing at the end of the lines to let him supply the rhyming words. Or try finding silly alternative rhymes!

- **Make up rhymes and jingles** about daily life – however silly!

- **Dance together** – play some music with a strong beat and let your hair down!

- **Sing action songs** – such as 'Heads and Shoulders, Knees and Toes'.
- **Make musical instruments**. Use small plastic bottles filled with rice, pasta and lentils for shakers. For drums, use wooden spoons or chopsticks to bang empty tins, paper plates or saucepans. Then use them to accompany a favourite CD or your own singing.

Listening to words

If your child has enjoyed joining in with rhymes, you may find he starts to make up his own – 'It's easy, weasy, peasy, deasy!' The words may not be proper words, but they show that he understands rhyme.

At this stage, your child still needs to hear lots of rhymes and songs, but he is now ready to start focusing on the sounds within words. Here are some more activities to try:

- Start a scrapbook and collect pictures of things beginning with different sounds.
- Play 'I spy'.
- Choose a letter and see how many things you can spot beginning with that sound.

Tip for helping your child with letters

It's important to remember the difference between letter *names* and letter *sounds*. For example: **H h** – 'aitch' – is the letter name, but 'huh' is the sound it makes.

Don't worry about writing words down just yet. The idea is to help your child to hear the individual sounds. Then when the time comes, he will be able to make the link between the sounds he hears and the written letters he sees.

Linking sounds and letters

Once your child can hear, say and remember a number of sounds, he may be able to start linking the sounds to letters or groups of letters. You'll know he's ready when he's pointing to words and saying things like, 'Look, that's a **d** – like in my name!' He may also start pointing out the similarities and differences between words when you are reading stories together.

At this point, you can help by talking about words when you are writing them down. The important thing is to remember that this process takes time and practice, so keep it light and fun. If he finds this difficult, stop straight away and just keep providing opportunities for him to *hear* and *say* the sounds.

Television

So what about listening to language on the television? Isn't that a good thing? Unfortunately not. Children learn language from interaction with real people, not from passively watching TV programmes. In fact, research has shown that children who watch a lot of TV are not as good at expressing themselves in spoken language. This is especially true when they watch a lot of programmes aimed at an older audience. (Also, lots of time in front of the screen contributes to children becoming unfit and overweight – which is not a good thing, either.)

This is not to say TV is a totally bad thing. Used in the right way, it does help to expand your child's knowledge of the world. And children, like adults, are entitled to relax and be entertained once in a while. But it pays to exercise control over your child's viewing. Here are some good rules of thumb for pre-schoolers:

- **Choose good quality programmes** – ones aimed specifically at young children, and preferably ones that you enjoy too.
- **Keep viewing to 20–30 minutes at a stretch** – and switch off when the programme has finished.
- **Do use and reuse favourite videos/DVDs** – children do benefit from seeing good programmes again.
- **Try to watch with your child** – and talk about the programme afterwards.
- **Keep TV as an activity for the family** – and don't be tempted to let your young child have one in his bedroom.
- **Keep TV out of mealtimes** – listen to each other instead.
- **Control what your child sees when other people are watching** – better to save your own TV programmes for when your child is tucked up in bed.
- **Don't let your child watch news programmes** – seeing repeated shots of catastrophes and distressing events may cause stress and anxiety.

W Of course, TV can be a lifesaver when you need a few minutes to do something important, or when you just need a break. But try not to use it as an electronic babysitter.

But we're telly addicts!

Let's face it, if you and your family are used to a lot of TV, it can be very very hard to reach for the off-switch. And in the short term, you may have a riot on your hands! But, as one parent said, whose whole family took part in a magazine challenge to give up TV for two weeks:

"The challenge has been tough… but so worthwhile. We have more time for other things, and TV has become a treat."

Writing and print

Young children do not know that print has meaning and that letters are different from pictures – they have to learn these things. They also need to learn what reading and writing are for, and how they help us in our daily lives.

Learning about print

Help your child to notice the print around him.

- **Draw your child's attention to print you see when you're out and about**, especially to words that have significance for him – *playground*, *ice creams*, *dinosaur*.

- **Look out for signs** like *stop*, *exit*, *open*, *closed* and *menu*. Talk about each sign and why it is there.

- **Get into the habit of letter spotting** – **P** for parking, **S** for salt and **P** for pepper, **H** and **C** on hot and cold taps, and so on.

- **Notice the print around your home** – on food packaging, clothes and household appliances.

ay, bee

- **Buy an alphabet book or alphabet frieze** (or make your own – see page 66). Refer to the letters by their alphabet names ('ay', 'bee', 'cee', etc) rather than their sounds ('kuh' for cat, etc). At this stage, it's about learning the alphabet rather than using the letters for reading.

Learning about writing

Take time to talk to your child about:

- your shopping list – invite him to offer his own ideas and let him see you writing them down;
- letters and cards to friends and family members;
- books and magazines that are important to you;
- 'To do' lists;
- emails you send;
- your diary and family calendar;
- labels you write.

ACTIVITY: The message board

Have a whiteboard as a family message board and use it to write reminders.

As well as helping your child to see how we can use writing to help organize our lives, it will get him thinking about past, present and future, and develop his concept of time.

Things to do.

Tom's birthday on Tuesday

Toilet rolls!

Phone Sue

Make lion mask with Ben

After a while, your child may be keen to help and will try and copy your writing. His first attempts may look pretty rough! But do praise his efforts, even if you think it just looks like scribble. (Otherwise he will be put right off making any further attempts.)

I've put cheese on the list.

Great. Thank you !

Developing writing

Writing is a complex skill that requires a lot of physical control. Before your child can manage the small movements required for handwriting, he must develop control over larger ones. You can help by providing activities that will help to develop his physical skills and co-ordination, such as:

- opportunities for climbing and balancing;
- toys that require hand–eye co-ordination, such as jigsaw puzzles and building bricks;
- opportunities to use cooking utensils;
- play dough and modelling clay.

Children's first attempts to make a mark usually involve moving food around a plate with their fingers. As they conduct further experiments, a few unwelcome marks may appear on walls and furniture! Try to provide lots of opportunities for drawing and painting, using a wide variety of materials.

In the early stages, the marks your child makes will just look like scribble – but it's all helping him learn hand control. At some point, he will understand the difference between drawing and writing, and will start to make shapes that look like letters.

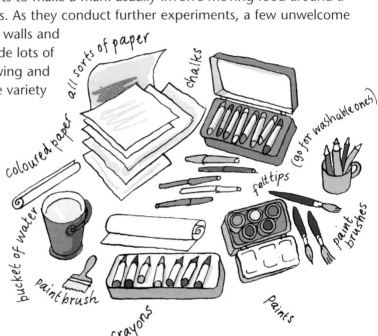

all sorts of paper

chalks

coloured paper

(go for washable ones)

felttips

paintbrushes

bucket of water

paintbrush

crayons

Paints

Tips for encouraging writing

If possible, provide a desk or a similar special place for writing. Equip it with different sorts of paper, stationery, pens, pencils, rulers, felt-tipped pens, crayons and pencil sharpeners. Add a clipboard, a hole punch, a glue-stick, an alphabet book, a picture dictionary.

Letter formation and pencil control

You may well find your child wants to write his name long before the teaching of writing begins in earnest. If your child is at school or in a pre-school setting, talk to the staff to see how they approach letter formation, and ask how you can help. Most provide guidance for parents, and some will give you a card with the alphabet or your child's name, showing the correct way to form each letter. This ensures your child won't get confused with conflicting instructions.

Around ... and up... and down.

Teach him to write the first letter of his name as a capital and the remaining letters in lower case.

Begin by skywriting (writing in the air) with his hand and forearm. Follow this by using a marker pen on a large piece of paper. (Washable marker pens are better than pencils in the early stages as they do not require as much pressure.) Then, after plenty of practice, let him try to write the letters with a pencil on a smaller piece of paper.

Tips for helping your child with writing

- Show him the correct way to hold the pencil. If he finds it difficult, place the pencil appropriately between his fingers and gently guide his hand as he writes.

- Holding a pencil puts a lot of pressure on the thumb and the first two fingers of the writing hand. If children are asked to write too much before these muscles are strong enough, writing can be physically painful, and if this happens they can lose their enthusiasm. So take care not to ask too much.

QUICK CHECK

✓ Read lots of books with your child.

✓ Learn rhymes and sing songs together.

✓ Don't let your young child sit for hours in front of the TV. Choose a few good quality programmes for him to watch.

✓ Draw your child's attention to the print all around him.

✓ Involve your child in the writing you do.

✓ Provide a wide variety of drawing and writing materials.

Off to School

Did you know...

? Research seems to show that from the age of three, most children benefit from having good quality pre-school education for a few hours a day?

? There is no rush for any child to begin 'formal' learning – the evidence shows that children who have good quality pre-school education, with lots of opportunity for play, tend to do better in the long run.

? There are several different types of pre-school provision – so you can choose what's best for you and your child.

CAN YOU REMEMBER?

Take a moment to think about your pre-school experience.

★ Do you remember going to any sort of class or group before you started primary school?

★ Do you remember what you did there?

★ Or did you stay at home until you started at primary school?

Whatever you remember of your own pre-school experience, your child's is likely to be quite different. Arrangements for pre-school children have changed considerably over recent years, and are changing still.

There are all sorts of options for your child's care and education before starting school. Your child does not have to have anything beyond what she is getting at home. However, research shows that most children who have had the experience of being in a good pre-school setting do find it easier to settle and make better progress when they start full-time education.

If you opt for some sort of pre-school care and education, there are many pathways that your child could take (see pages 94–95). What is available to your child will vary according to where you live, what work or other commitments you might have, and maybe what budget you have. It's up to you to choose the path that best suits your child and your family.

The pre-school stage is extremely important because it's when children are laying the foundations for everything that follows. Those who teach children in this 'foundation stage' aim to build on everything children have already learned at home. They work closely with parents to give all young children, including those with special needs, the best possible start in life.

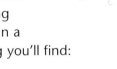

Good early years education is based on comprehensive research into how young children learn best. So in a good pre-school setting you'll find:

- lots of play and first-hand experience;
- great emphasis on developing communication skills – which are crucial to success in reading and writing;
- sessions that take account of young children's need for frequent physical activity;
- priority given to children's personal, emotional and social development;
- learning that builds on what each child can already do – and allows for the fact that this varies from child to child.

The curriculum in the foundation stage is somewhat different to that in the later years. Rather than having traditional subjects such as English, mathematics and science, the curriculum is organized into areas of learning:

 Personal, social and emotional development

 Communication, language and literacy

 Mathematical development

 Knowledge and understanding of the world

 Physical development

 Creative development

Choosing a pre-school setting

Pre-school settings are only as good as the people who manage them and work in them, and quality can vary. There are also many different types of provision. (See pages 94–96 for details of how this works in the UK.)

It's a good idea to research what's on offer in your area and to start early, as different places have varying systems for applications and some might have waiting lists. Find out the timetable for applications at places in your area well before it's time to make the decision.

When you've found out about the possible options, phone to arrange some visits. There may be set days or times for this, or you may be able to arrange an individual tour. Try to go when the children are there, and do take your own child with you. Obviously, every pre-school setting will be eager to tell you how wonderful they are! So it will help if you gather your ideas about exactly what you want to find out before you go. You might like to make a list along these lines:

Things to observe

- Is everyone friendly and welcoming?
- Are the children generally calm, safe, happy and playing together well?
- Are the staff interacting with the children and joining in with their play? (And if you've taken your own child with you, how do they welcome and interact with her?)
- Do staff listen carefully to what the children say and talk to them respectfully?
- Are they managing the children's behaviour in a positive way?
- Is the environment safe, clean and secure – both indoors and out?
- Is it welcoming and stimulating?
- Is there enough space for children to be active?
- Are there comfy places where children can rest and relax?

Questions you might want to ask:

- What is the ratio of children to staff?
- Will my child meet the same adults every time she attends? Is there a key-worker system, so that she will have one 'special' adult with overall responsibility for her?
- What qualifications and experience do the staff have?
- How will I get to know about what my child is learning? And are there ways I can get involved in the process?
- How will you share information about my child's progress?
- How do you communicate with parents who are working and may not be the adult who drops off and picks up the child?
- Will there always be someone available to talk to if I have any worries or concerns?
- What are the procedures for confidentiality and privacy, and for emergencies?
- What happens if my child is ill while she is here?
- What will you do if she is distressed?
- Can parents obtain a copy of the curriculum?
- How are activities planned to meet the curriculum?
- What resources and equipment are available to support children's learning?
- What meals are served, and are special diets catered for?
- How are any special needs met?
- What are the opening times and dates?
- Is there an information booklet or prospectus that I can take away?
- (In some circumstances) What is the cost of attendance? Are there any additional costs that could arise?

Making the choice

It can be helpful to talk to parents of children already at the pre-school setting about their experience. Keep in mind, though, that different people can have different experiences of a setting for all sorts of reasons. As you weigh up all the points for and against each option, listen also to your gut feelings. Does the place feel good to you? Can you see your child there?

Choosing a school

Although it might seem quite early, around your child's third birthday is probably the time to start thinking about primary school. You may even want to consider primary education options at the time that you research pre-school provision, in order to plan for a smooth transition from one stage to the next. If you have a choice between two or more schools, gather information as soon as you can, so that you have enough time to make an informed decision. In order to find out more about individual schools you might want to:

- Get a copy of the school's prospectus or information pack.
- Visit the school website.
- **W** Look up any reports on the school.
- Talk to parents of children at the school (again, bearing in mind that different families have different experiences for all sorts of reasons).
- And, most importantly, make an appointment to visit.

Just as with choosing an early years setting, it almost certainly helps to think about exactly what you want to find out before you visit. Here's another similar list, this time for a school fact-finding mission.

Things to observe

- Does the school feel friendly and welcoming?
- Are the children generally polite and well behaved?
- Do they seem happy and absorbed in what they're doing?
- How do staff interact with children? Do they talk to them respectfully and listen carefully to what they say?
- Do the classrooms look attractive, stimulating, well equipped and well organized?
- Is children's work attractively displayed? Does it look purposeful and interesting?

Try to look at the school prospectus or information pack before you go, then you can concentrate on finding out anything that isn't covered in there. This might include:

Things to find out

- Are parents welcome in the school? What opportunities are there to be involved? Do parents help in classrooms, for example?
- How will I find out what my child is learning?
- What facilities does the school have for sport? technology? music?
- What is the school's approach to behaviour and discipline?
- What size are the classes, and how many teaching assistants or other helpers does each class have?
- What clubs and activities are available in school and after school?
- What links does the school have with the local community?
- How are any special needs met?
- What provision is there for before or after school care for children with working parents?
- How does the school communicate with parents?

Making the choice

Choosing a school for your child is a big decision – she's going to be there for between six and seven hours a day, five days a week. In addition to all the pros and cons of the school itself, you may also need to consider distance...

The local school

- Getting a place should not be a problem
- Your child's school friends are more likely to live nearby – much more convenient for playing together after school
- Less travelling, more walking and cycling – healthier all round
- The school may have good links with your local community

The not-so-local school

- Check the admission rules – is there a reasonable chance of a place?
- School friends may not live nearby – your child's social life may be trickier to manage
- More travelling, more sitting in traffic queues or on buses
- The school may have good links with the local community – but not yours

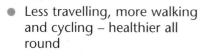

...but in the end, it comes down to what feels right for your child.

QUICK CHECK

✓ There are many options for early education, and you can choose the pathway that best meets your family's needs.

✓ Children who have had a good early education find starting school easier.

✓ When choosing a setting or school, gather as much information as you can – and then don't be afraid to trust your gut feelings.

A New Chapter

Did you know...

? There are lots of ways you can help prepare your child for school?

? For some children, the first year of school can be very tiring?

? One of the best ways to support your child at school is simply to talk about it and show an interest?

THE BEST DAYS OF YOUR LIFE? OR NOT?

Take a moment to think back to your own experience of starting school.

Can you remember your first day? What happened and what did it feel like?

Who was your first teacher, and what was he or she like?

What good things can you remember about your first year at school?

What worried or distressed you?

What things can you remember doing in class?

What was it like when you went into the playground? Did you have friends to play with? What did you play?

What were lunchtimes like? Did you have a school lunch or a packed lunch?

If possible, compare your experiences with your partner or a friend.

Remembering how you felt can help you to understand what your child is facing. Also, be aware of how your feelings about school could affect your child.

Was your overall experience positive? That's great. You'll probably find it easy to be positive about school with your child. But don't assume that your child will necessarily find it easy just because you did.

Was your overall experience not very positive? Take care that it doesn't affect the way you talk about school to your child. And it doesn't mean your child will find it hard.

Either way, you'll almost certainly find things have changed since you were in the classroom.

Preparing for school

Even if your child has coped well with pre-school education, starting school is a big step. He'll be there for a much larger part of the day – including lunchtimes – and he'll be learning as part of a larger group. Your child will need to be that bit more independent. You can help him by making sure that by the time he goes to school, he can:

- hang his coat and bag on a hook;

- go to the toilet by himself;

- wash and dry his hands;

- pack and unpack his bag;

- open his lunchbox and eat his lunch in the right order;

- blow his nose;

- manage his clothing;

- put on his socks and shoes;

- take turns;

- follow simple instructions, for example: stand behind, in front, next to; put it underneath, on top, in the middle, and so on;

- follow a short sequence of instructions;

- be able to ask clearly when he wants something or needs help.

It will also help if he can recognize his own name, so he'll be able to identify named items (like a lunchbox or clothes) that belong to him.

Getting the idea

Going to school is a big change. As well as making sure that your child can manage his shoes and go to the toilet, you can increase his confidence by letting him know what to expect and helping him to look forward to it.

- If your child is in a pre-school setting in the area, find out how they liaise with the school and support children through the transition.
- Be positive and enthusiastic about school (even if you feel a bit anxious): 'You'll do lots of exciting things.' 'You'll make new friends.'
- If your child seems worried by the idea of school, don't dismiss his worries. Gently encourage him to talk about them so you can find out exactly what he's afraid of – and then provide reassurance.
- Use every opportunity for your child to familiarize himself with the school. There may be school welcome days, home visits from staff, booklets of information and activities sent home. If the school has a website, you may be able to look at photos of school life and events, and perhaps contributions from children.

- Talk about the kind of things that will happen and what school routines are like.
- Make sure your child knows the teacher's name, and the name and whereabouts of his class
- Make sure he knows who he can go to if he's worried.
- It may help if your child knows some other children starting at the same time. If you don't know anyone already, you could try and make contact with another family. The school may be able to help put you in touch.

The first few days

When your child starts school, he may well begin with mornings only and gradually build up to a full day after a couple of weeks or so. This can be a tricky period for working parents. Some people manage to juggle with a combination of parents and relatives doing the taking and collecting. Others find it easiest to take some leave over the transition period and enjoy being with their child over this milestone. When the first day finally arrives:

Try to have everything well organized, so you can take things calmly. Avoid rush, but not breakfast.

When you arrive at school, you may be able to stay with your child for a little while.

When the time comes to leave, don't sneak off while he is absorbed in an activity, but say a quick, cheerful goodbye.

Of course, this is unbelievably hard if your child is upset or clinging on to you. But be firm about your farewell, reassuring him that you will be back to collect him at lunchtime.

Many parents are surprised by how tiring school can be. Even children who were used to being in some form of day care or at a pre-school setting can be quite exhausted by the first few weeks of school. If possible, let your child have some down-time when you get home. Snuggling on the sofa with a favourite video is probably just the thing.

The first year – or so
Get involved

Research shows that when parents are involved in their child's school, children do better. Most schools are very keen to have parents in to help with classroom activities. It's a great opportunity to see what goes on in school and to get to know your child's teacher and classmates. Children generally like having their parent in their class, but if yours does not you might still be able to help out in another class. If you work during school hours or have younger children, helping on a regular basis may not be possible. But you might be able arrange to join in with trips or special activities.

Deal with worries

Many parents have worries about their child at some point during the first year. Most things sort themselves out quite quickly, but if you have ongoing concerns then the best thing is to talk to the teacher. You may be able to catch him or her at the beginning of the day, but often they are setting things up and welcoming the children. A good approach can be to send a brief note with your child to say that there's something you'd like to talk about. Then the teacher may suggest a time when you can go in, or they may be able to phone you.

Teachers are busy, but they are also concerned about your child's education and will be keen to hear about any concerns you may have. You are the expert on your child: good teachers know this and are keen to work with parents.

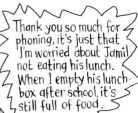

Thank you so much for phoning, it's just that I'm worried about Jamil not eating his lunch. When I empty his lunchbox after school, it's still full of food.

If it's all too much...

School takes a huge amount of physical, mental and emotional energy. In the first few months your child may become very tired, especially if he is one of the younger ones in the class. He may need a shorter school day just for a little while. If you feel that he's not coping, talk to your child's teacher – and be prepared to explain what's happening at home. Some children can confuse the issue by holding it all together beautifully while they're at school, only to be whining and throwing yogurt at the wall by five o'clock.

Home time

When your child comes home from school, he may be eager to talk about his school day. But if not, don't pressurize him. You may find him willing to talk later on, perhaps after a meal or in the bath. If so, let him know that you are interested in what he's been doing, and ask questions that

encourage him to reflect: 'What did you learn?' 'What did you think about that?'

Your after-school routine may depend partly on the requirements and activities of the rest of your family. But if possible, allow your child to unwind from his day in the way that meets his needs – whether it's a quiet activity at the table or a run-around to let off steam. As your child gets to school age, there may be opportunities to start all sorts of extra activities. Again, some children may take it all in their stride, but for many it may be best to wait a while before starting on a round of after-school clubs and classes.

Your child may start bringing a reading book home. Find a time when you can sit quietly together to enjoy the reading without interruption.

You will probably see a difference in your child. He may seem suddenly quite grown up. Or he may regress and start behaving like a toddler again. Either is quite normal and part of adjusting to the change.

Congratulations! Your child is now in 'full-time education'. Of course, he's been in full-time education since he arrived to live with you. And you and your family will continue to play a vital role in his education for many years to come. Remember, as you go through those years, that all any parent can do is their best. So don't waste your energy trying to be perfect. Making mistakes is an inevitable part of being human. So when you do get it wrong:

- Don't waste time and effort beating yourself up.
- Accept that you did the best you could with the knowledge and experience that you had at the time.
- Save your energy for doing something about the things you want to change.
- Understand that children will forgive us almost anything, as long as they know that we love them.

And finally, know that there is nothing worse for a child than a 'perfect parent'. They learn so much more from parents who can own their mistakes, admit them – and then do things differently because of those mistakes.

QUICK CHECK

- ✓ Prepare your child for school by letting him know what to expect.
- ✓ Make sure he is able to do all the things he'll need to in order to look after himself and his belongings.
- ✓ Be sensitive to his changing needs during the first year.
- ✓ If you can, get involved with your child's school.

Resources

Picture books

There are lots of really good picture books to choose from; here are some tried and tested favourites you might like to look out for.

Holes and flaps
The Very Hungry Caterpillar Eric Carle (Puffin)
Where's Spot? (and other Spot books) Eric Hill (Puffin)

Rhyme and repetition
Each Peach Pear Plum Janet and Alan Ahlberg (Puffin)
Hairy Maclary from Donaldson's Dairy Lynley Dodd (Puffin)
This is the Bear Sarah Hayes and Helen Craig (Walker)
Mr Magnolia Quentin Blake (Red Fox)

Home and community life
Alfie Gets in First Shirley Hughes (Red Fox)
Dogger Shirley Hughes (Picture Lions)
So Much Trish Cooke (Walker Books)
Amazing Grace Mary Hoffman (Frances Lincoln)
Billy's Sunflower Nicola Moon (Little Hippo)
Dear Daddy Phillipe Dupasquier (Puffin)
Handa's Surprise Eileen Browne (Walker)
It Was Jake Anita Jeram (Walker Books)
Jamaica and Brianna Juanita Havill (Mammoth)
Tall Inside Jean Richardson (Puffin)
Hector's New Trainers Amanda Vesey (Picture Lions)
The Time It Took Tom Nick Sharratt (Scholastic)
Pass It, Polly Sarah Garland (Puffin)
Through My Window Tony Bradman and Eileen Browne (Mammoth)

Fantasy and fun
Funnybones Janet and Alan Ahlberg (Puffin)
Angry Arthur Oram and Satsoshi Kitamura (Red Fox)
Mr Gumpy's Outing John Burningham (Red Fox)
Not Now Bernard David McKee (Red Fox)
Pass the Jam Jim Kaye Umansky and Margaret Chamberlain (Red Fox)

The Elephant and the Bad Baby Elfrida Vipont and Raymond Briggs (Puffin)
Where the Wild Things Are Maurice Sendak (Red Fox)
Where's My Teddy? Jez Alborough (Walker)

All sorts of animals

Brown Bear, Brown Bear, What Do You See? Bill Martin Jnr and Eric Carl (Puffin)
Danny's Duck June Crebbin (Walker)
Dear Zoo Rod Campbell (Puffin)
Doctor Dog Babette Cole (Red Fox)
Duck in the Truck Jez Alborough (Collins)
Elmer David McKee (Red Fox)
Farmer Duck Martin Waddell (Walker)
Gorilla Anthony Browne (Red Fox)
Little Rabbit Foo Foo Michael Rosen and Arthur Robbins (Walker)
My Cat Likes to Hide in Boxes Eve Sutton and Lynley Dodd (Puffin)
One Snowy Night Nick Butterworth (Collins)
Owl Babies Martin Waddell (Walker)
Peace at Last Jill Murphy (Macmillan)
Rosie's Walk Pat Hutchins (Red Fox)
Solo Paul Geraghty (Hutchinson)
Suddenly Colin McNaughton (Collins)
The Bear Under The Stairs Helen Cooper (Corgi)
The Gingerbread Boy Ian Beck (Oxford University Press)
The Tiger Who Came to Tea Judith Kerr (Collins)
Tortoise's Dream Joanna Troughton (Puffin)
We're Going on a Bear Hunt Michael Rosen and Helen Oxenbury (Walker)

Non-fiction

Again, there are a lot of good non-fiction books for young children. Choose ones about subjects that you know will interest your child.

Audio CDs and cassettes

Pudding and Pie (cassette) Oxford University Press
Oranges and Lemons (cassette) Oxford University Press
Playsongs CDs **www.playsongs.co.uk**

Useful websites

Page 36
www.healthyliving.gov.uk A very user-friendly site giving advice on healthy eating, including helpful tips and lots of recipes and ideas for meals, snacks and lunchboxes.

www.mypyramid.gov Highly interactive US website with healthy eating advice and good kids' pages.

Page 42
www.sleepforkids.org Kid-friendly site run by the US National Sleep Foundation.

Page 52
www.2simple.com Well designed software for young children, with the emphasis on creativity.

Page 58
www.planet-science.com Fantastic and very jazzy science-for-kids site with lots of great links.

www.24hourmuseum.org.uk Information about museums, galleries, exhibitions and events in your area. Zone for kids has links to children's pages on museum websites, organized by topic.

Page 70
www.literacytrust.org.uk Really good advice on using TV with children, plus lots of other excellent information and resources for parents.

Page 80
www.ofsted.gov.uk/reports/ The Ofsted website where you can read the Ofsted inspection report for any school in England.

Ideas for Chapter 2

No 'correct answers', of course. But you could say something along the lines of:

"The video instructions do seem complicated. I need to find someone who can show me what to do."

"Jay seems to be having a hard time at the moment. I wonder what would help him?"

"I passed on everything except for reversing, so I'll need to do some more work on that before I take my test again."

Pre-school pathways in the UK

 Private, voluntary or independent nursery

 Children's centre

 Registered childminder

 Playgroups, 'Stay and play', etc

Foundation Stage

Your child is entitled to a place at a registered 'setting', which could be a...

Primary school

Private, voluntary or independent nursery

Reception

Year 1

Children's centre

Accredited childminder

Primary schools take children into the Reception class during the year they have their fifth birthday

Playgroup

Maintained (state) nursery

Nursery class in a Primary school

Foundation Stage unit

The UK school and pre-school system

In the UK, there is a wide variety of pre-school care and education available to your child. This can take place in any of a number of different **settings**:

These include:

- state-run nursery classes and nursery schools;
- private nurseries;
- pre-school playgroups;
- accredited childminders who are part of an approved network;
- children's centres;
- Foundation Stage units in primary schools.

Children aged 3–5 are in a phase of education called the **Foundation Stage**. Under current UK law, every three and four year old is entitled to free, part-time nursery education for up to six terms before they reach their fifth birthday. 'Part-time' means up to 12.5 hours a week.

Children are not legally required to start full-time education until the term after their fifth birthday, although many primary schools take children into their Reception class during the year in which they reach their fifth birthday. So many children begin their primary education when they are four. However, they are still in the Foundation Stage.

The Foundation Stage is the first of several key stages in the UK education system. Full details of the Foundation Stage curriculum are available on the QCA website:

http://www.qca.org.uk

Other useful sites for finding and choosing childcare, nurseries and schools:

www.parentscentre.gov.uk

www.direct.gov.uk/EducationAndLearning

www.surestart.gov.uk

And finally:
www.ace-ed.org.uk/advice/jargon.html
An a–z of educational jargon – everything you wanted to know about those strange terms but were too afraid to ask!